ALL FOR THE BETTER
A Story of El Barrio

by Nicholasa Mohr

Alex Haley, General Editor

Illustrations by Rudy Gutierrez

STECK-VAUGHN COMPANY
ELEMENTARY • SECONDARY • ADULT • LIBRARY

For Evelina's sisters, Lillian Lopez and Elba Cabrera, and her daughter, Lorraine Montenegro, as they carry forth her legacy.

Published by Steck-Vaughn Company.

Text, illustrations, and cover art copyright © 1993 by Dialogue Systems, Inc., 79 Fifth Avenue, New York, New York 10003. All rights reserved.

Cover art by Rudy Gutierrez

Printed in the United States of America
    8 9 10 LB 05 04 03 02 01 00

Library of Congress Cataloging-in-Publication Data

Mohr, Nicholasa.
    All for the better: a story of El Barrio / Nicholasa Mohr; illustrated by Rudy Gutierrez.
        p. cm.—(Stories of America)
    ISBN 0-8114-7220-5 (hardcover) — ISBN 0-8114-8060-7 (softcover)
    1. Antonetty, Evelina, 1922–1984—Juvenile literature. 2. Puerto Ricans—New York (N.Y.)—Biography—Juvenile literature. 3. Puerto Ricans—New York (N.Y.)—Social conditions—Juvenile literature. 4. New York (N.Y.)—Biography—Juvenile literature. I. Gutierrez, Rudy, ill. II. Title. III. Series.
F128.9.P85M62 1993
974.7'100468729502—dc20
    [B]   92-23639
                                                                        CIP
                                                                        AC
ISBN 0-8114-7220-5 (Hardcover)
ISBN 0-8114-8060-7 (Softcover)

A Note About Alex Haley

All for the Better is one of two books in the *Stories of America* series completed after the death of Alex Haley in February 1992.

Despite his involvement in a number of other projects, Mr. Haley found the time to guide the formation of the *Stories of America*. As General Editor, he provided editorial direction through all stages of book development. And for each of the 26 books completed prior to his death, he wrote a special introduction.

Alex Haley was an inspiration to all of us involved in the project. We did our best to carry on in his spirit. We hope that readers will find evidence of Alex Haley's influence on these pages, just as we felt his influence while completing them.

The *Stories of America* series is Alex Haley's contribution to the education of America's young people. This book is respectfully dedicated to his memory.

Introduction

Some people live to make a difference. However they find the world around them, they try to make it better. For them, nothing is so perfect it can't be improved, and no problem is so difficult it can't be faced.

This is a story about a young girl who in a small way made a difference to many people in her community. She had no special gift beyond caring, but you will see how much you can do when you care enough to make a difference.

Contents

Chapter 1 Leaving Home   **1**

Chapter 2 Speak English   **14**

Chapter 3 People Are Hungry   **23**

Chapter 4 *Uno, Dos, Tres*   **38**

Epilogue   **46**

Afterword   **53**

Notes   **54**

1 LEAVING HOME

Cuidate mi hijita. "Take good care of yourself, my little daughter." It was September 11, 1933, and eleven-year-old Evelina Lopez was leaving her family for the first time. Evelina struggled to hold back her tears as she said good-bye. She asked for her mother's blessing. *Bendición Mami,* she whispered.

Her mother held her a long time, then said, "Be brave, my sweet Evelina. God willing, we will all be together someday. I promise."

Her mother, Eva Cruz Lopez, had faced an impossible decision—to part with her oldest daughter. Eva Lopez was raising three children by herself. In ordinary years that is hard enough to do, but in the years of the Great Depression it had become a hopeless task.

Worried about her children's future, Eva Lopez decided to send Evelina to live in New York City with Eva's older sister, Vicenta. Vicenta had recently married. She and her husband had no children yet and were willing to take Evelina in to help the family. The Depression had brought hard times to New York City, but things were much worse in Puerto Rico. Sending Evelina to live with her Tía Vicenta was the best thing to do.

Evelina kissed her little sisters, eight-year-old Lillian and baby Elba, for the last time.

"You will grow so fast, little Elba," Evelina said sadly to her baby sister. "I won't be able to see you take your first steps."

She kissed baby Elba again as the ship's shrill whistle blew. It was time to board. Evelina had to hurry. She hugged Lillian and then her mother. "I'll miss my best friend and sister and you, too, Mami. I'll miss all of you so much and think of you every day."

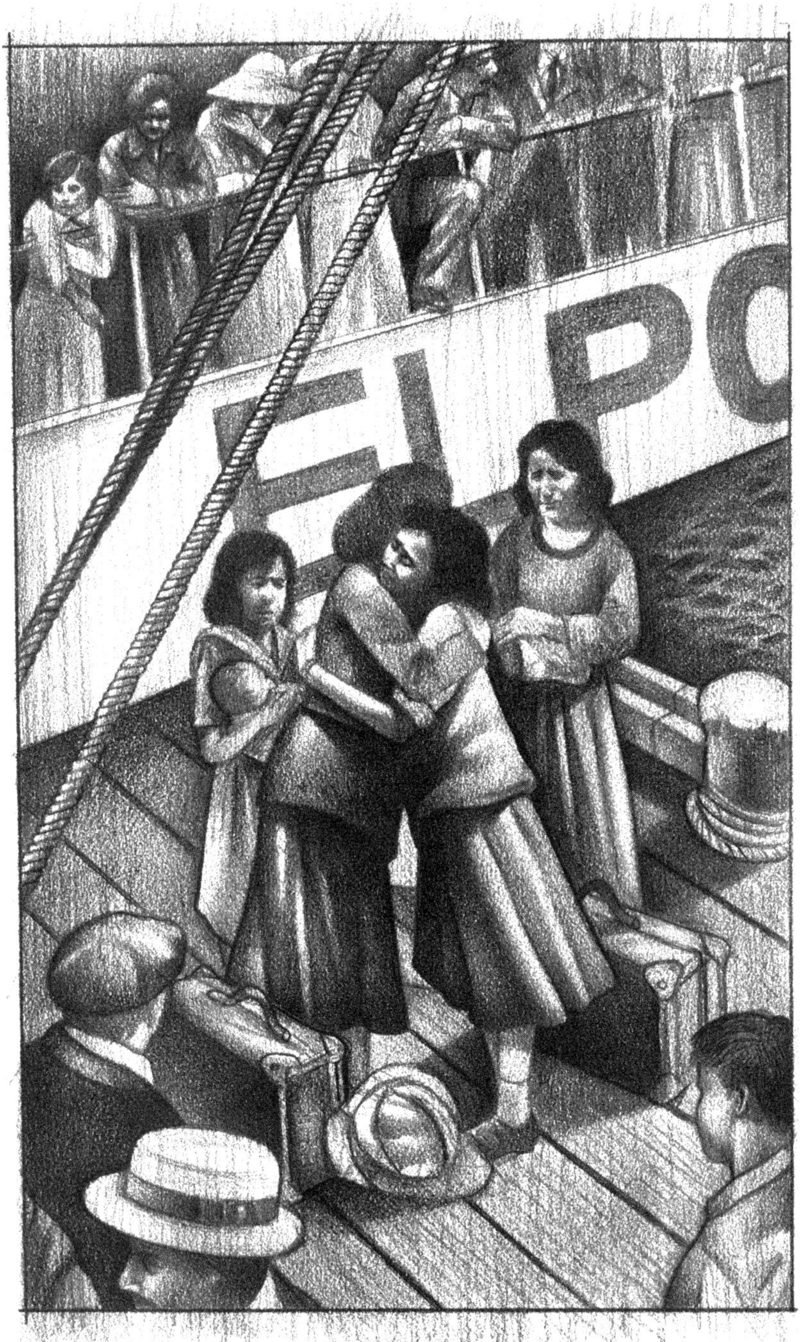
EL PO

Then she rushed to board the ship *El Ponce,* which was ready to embark on its five-day journey across the sea to New York City. Once on the ship, Evelina quickly made her way through all the people crowded on the deck and reached the railing. She looked down on the docks where people were waving good-bye to their relatives.

Evelina saw her mother and sister. They waved farewell to her. She grasped the railing, and leaning forward, waved and blew kisses in their direction.

The shrill whistle blared again as the ship slowly pulled away from the dock and out into San Juan Harbor. Evelina watched as first her mother and sisters and then her beautiful Island disappeared from view. Soon the soft green-blue of the Caribbean Sea and the cloudless bright sunny sky were all she was able to see.

She wondered if she would ever again see the abundant flowers and tall palm trees glistening in the bright sunshine. Would she ever again bathe in Puerto Rico's blue waters or walk along its white sandy beaches? Would she ever again bask in the warmth of her beautiful tropical Island of Puerto Rico? It was scary to think the answer to these questions might be no.

But the scariest part was being without her family. Evelina hardly remembered her Tía Vicenta, who had left Puerto Rico several years earlier. And she had never even met her aunt's new husband. She felt as if she was going to live with strangers. Evelina tried hard not to be too fearful about the future. Mami, she told herself, had done what was best for *la familia*. So she would do what she must to be brave.

Doña Clara, an acquaintance of her mother's, was also sailing on *El Ponce*. She had agreed to share a cabin with Evelina and to take charge of her during their voyage.

During the first day at sea, Doña Clara was very attentive. She saw to it that Evelina was safely settled in her bunk and had all she needed to be comfortable. But the following day the sea grew rough and Doña Clara became seasick. She remained sick the entire voyage and never once left their cramped little cabin.

It was Evelina who ended up taking care of Doña Clara. "You're an angel," Doña Clara whispered from her sickbed. "I'm the one who is supposed to take care of you." Then she insisted that Evelina mingle with the other passengers. Since Doña Clara slept most of the time, Evelina took her advice. But she always checked in on Doña Clara to make sure she was all right.

Everyone remarked on what a thoughtful and responsible girl Evelina was. Her outgoing personality and good looks endeared her to all she met. "Evelina, come have dinner with us," they would say. Or, "Evelina, join us for a game of checkers." She was always sought after, and by the time the journey was over, Evelina had made many friends on board ship.

To her surprise, on the last day of the voyage Evelina felt sad. Sad about leaving *El Ponce*. Sad about saying goodbye to Doña Clara and all her new friends. Everyone had been so kind! They had taken her mind away from her own sorrow. They had made the separation from her mother and sisters seem less terrible, less fearful.

But now the voyage was coming to an end. Evelina came up on deck. With all her might she wished that *El Ponce* was entering San Juan Harbor, not New York Harbor. She wanted to be back in Puerto Rico.

Evelina watched as this strange new city loomed gray and forbidding. She cringed at the sight of the tall buildings crowding across the horizon. Her heart sank as she looked around. The city skies were dreary. The water had a foul, oily smell.

A tug guided *El Ponce* to the dock. Evelina watched the workmen move around the dock shouting strange words at one another. They looped heavy ropes from the ship around the dock's iron posts. Quickly *El Ponce* was tied fast and the five-day journey was over. Doña

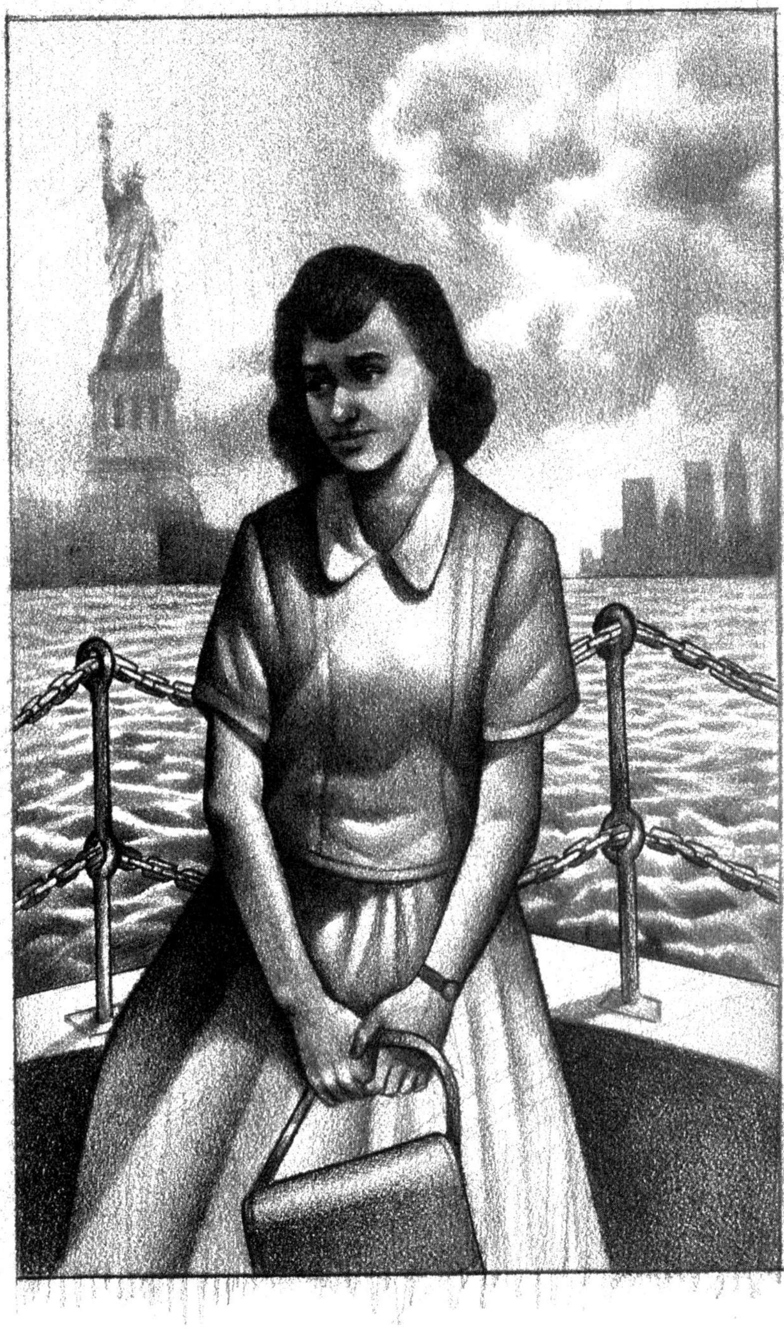

Clara, who had recovered as soon as they had neared land again, took Evelina's hand to lead her ashore. They went down the gangplank onto the docks of South Brooklyn.

"Now I must make sure that you find your aunt and uncle," she said. Many of the passengers hugged Evelina. "Keep in touch," they said. *Que Dios te bendiga.* "God bless," they said.

"Wait here and don't move," said Doña Clara. "First, I have to make sure we have all our luggage. Then we'll find your aunt and uncle."

Evelina stood by herself and waited in these strange new surroundings. She watched as everyone bustled about, gathering their luggage and looking for their kinfolk. Suddenly she felt lost and bewildered. Where was Doña Clara? Where was Tía Vicenta? She was close to tears when she heard her name being called.

"Evelina! Evelina! Here we are!" She turned to see her Tía Vicenta waving eagerly in her direction. Beside her aunt stood a man who must be her new uncle. He, too, was waving at her.

Her aunt gave her a great big hug. "This," she said, "is Enrique Godreau, my husband and your uncle. But everybody calls him Godreau."

Godreau smiled at his new niece.

"Your Tío Godreau is glad to see that you did not get seasick, fall overboard, and get eaten by sharks," her uncle said with a wink. "So you must be as smart and as tough as your aunt!" Evelina had to laugh and immediately felt less sad.

Meanwhile, Doña Clara had returned with the luggage. Vicenta and Doña Clara knew each other from Puerto Rico. They greeted each other warmly. "You have a very special niece there," said Doña Clara. "Evelina will bring joy to your life."

Doña Clara's brother and his wife were somewhere in the growing crowd on the dock. She had to go find them. Before she left she gave Evelina a long hug. Everyone quickly exchanged addresses and then said good-bye.

A little while later, Evelina took her first ride on a New York City subway. The crowded subway crossed a bridge and then rode high above the streets on its way to Spanish Harlem. Evelina had to hold her ears when the train shrieked its way around turns. She stared out the window at the vast city filled with brick and concrete buildings.

The train rumbled uptown until they reached their stop. Her aunt and uncle had an apartment on 117th Street and Madison Avenue. "Here we are in *El Barrio*," said her aunt. "Home at last."

The community of Spanish Harlem was called *El Barrio,* which means "The Neighborhood." *El Barrio* was the largest community of Spanish-speaking people in New York City. The majority of these people were Puerto Ricans. And most of them were newly arrived from the Island, just like Evelina.

There were no skyscrapers here, and most of the buildings were not so very tall. Just like home, small shops lined the avenues. Grocery stores were called *bodegas.* Even bakeries and luncheonettes had Spanish names, *Bodega de Santurce* and *Rivera's Luncheonette—Comidas Criollas.* There were also *botánicas,* which sold religious articles just like the ones back in Puerto Rico. Evelina felt more at ease. *El Barrio* had a familiar feeling.

"Here's our building," said her uncle. "Now instead of climbing a hill like we do back home, we climb lots of steps."

Evelina followed as they went up three flights of stairs.

"Welcome," said her aunt, holding the door to their small apartment open. "This is your home." She took Evelina to her bedroom. "Someday, God willing, your mother and sisters will be here with us, too."

Evelina settled down in her small bedroom. She put away her few items of clothing and gently placed the photographs of her mother and sisters on her bureau. She missed them so much her heart ached. Her eyes brimmed with tears.

Evelina wiped away her tears and stood looking out her bedroom window. Outside, traffic filled the streets and people scurried around in every direction. She wondered if they also missed home and if they were away from their families, too. Maybe some of them would be going back someday.

She saw a woman walking with two girls about the same ages as Lillian and herself. All three held hands. They are happy and they are together, she thought.

"Please, dear God," she prayed, "if I am never to go back to my beloved Puerto Rico, then, like Tía Vicenta says, bring Mami, Lillian, and baby Elba here to me soon."

Evelina understood that no matter what happened in her future, right now she was starting a brand-new life.

2 SPEAK ENGLISH

In *El Barrio* school had already started. So one morning, just a few days after she arrived, Evelina found herself seated in a big classroom with a tall ceiling and heavy, ink-stained desks.

At first, it was hard to understand the teachers because they only spoke English. But Evelina was smart and a very fast learner. Soon she was speaking English well enough to make friends.

Her first friend was a pretty little girl named Sarah. Sarah, who reminded Evelina of Lillian, was always by her side. She and

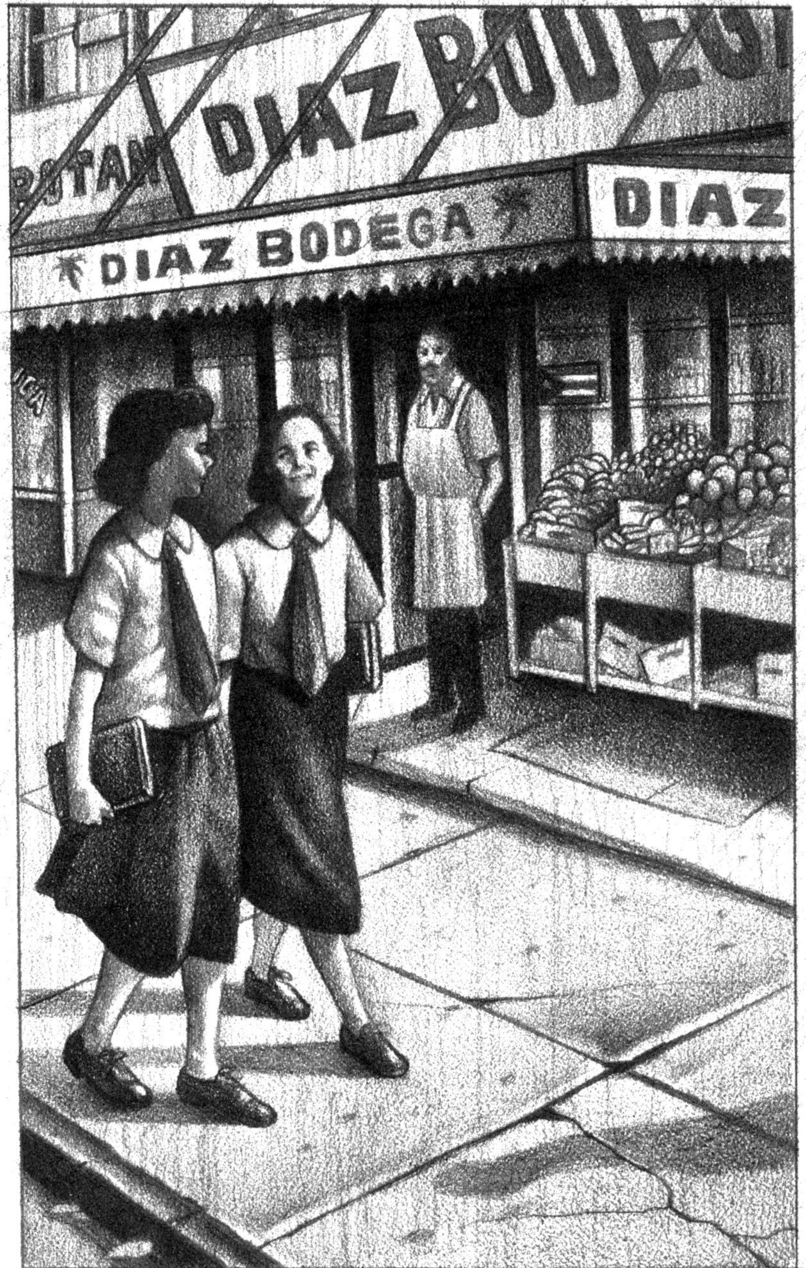
DIAZ
DIAZ BODEGA
DIAZ

Evelina ate lunch together at school and walked home together. Sarah helped Evelina with her English, too. All was going well with her new school and her new friend.

But about two months after she started school, near the end of November, Evelina began to scratch her head constantly. It itched something awful. Finally, her aunt examined her hair.

"My goodness!" cried Tía Vicenta, "You've got lice!" Actually, Evelina was not totally surprised. That same week at school Sarah had been sent home because she had head lice.

"I must have caught them from Sarah," explained Evelina. Her aunt went to the pharmacy and bought the necessary medicine. She cleaned Evelina's hair and then cut off her long dark curls.

"Now your head is clean," said her aunt. "And your hair is short enough so that we can easily see if it gets infected again."

"But, Evelina, are you sure you wanted to get rid of those lice?" asked Tío Godreau.

"After all, these are American lice and they speak English!"

But Evelina was used to Godreau's teasing. "Tío," she responded, "my English is much better. I don't think I need these lice anymore."

Godreau shook his head and laughed. His niece was certainly learning fast!

At school, too, Evelina was one of the brightest students in class. Her favorite subject was history. She read constantly. Evelina was often called upon to help the teacher.

This special attention pleased Evelina, but not all her classmates shared her delight. Soon she was considered to be a teacher's pet. Some of her classmates didn't like her because of this. Others didn't like her because she was from Puerto Rico. Classmates, white and black, made fun of her Spanish accent. In her town in Puerto Rico, people of all colors—black, brown, and tan—all lived like family. Here everything seemed different, and Evelina didn't understand why.

Two black girls especially disliked Evelina. One was the class bully. The bully threatened Evelina, and both girls made fun of the way she spoke English. Evelina was afraid of them and complained to her aunt.

For the next few days, Tía Vicenta met Evelina after school and walked her safely home. This kept Evelina from getting beat up after school but didn't end her problems with the two girls. They stayed on the lookout for Evelina.

Meeting Evelina after school was difficult for her aunt. She was busy working and taking care of the household. After a while she decided that Evelina would have to solve the problem on her own.

"You must learn to handle yourself," Tía Vicenta said. "I cannot be picking you up at school every day and protecting you like a baby. Learn to fight back or take the consequences." Her aunt's word was final.

The next day after school, the bully and her friend waited for Evelina.

"Hey, girl!" shouted the bully, who was

taller and stronger than Evelina. "I got something to say to you." Evelina tried to walk away, but the bully's friend blocked her path. "You ain't going nowhere, spick girl."

Evelina snapped. She was tired of being afraid, tired of being abused because she was Puerto Rican. Evelina dropped her books on the sidewalk. Instantly, classmates gathered around them and waited.

"Don't call me names," warned Evelina.

The bully stepped up to Evelina and gave her a fierce shove. Evelina lost her balance and fell.

"Go on and whip her!" laughed the bully's friend.

Then as the bully lurched forward, Evelina jumped up and rammed her head right into the bully's stomach. As her anger took over, Evelina began fighting back. Her classmates cheered Evelina on against the bully. In no time the bully was crying. Finally, several adults who were passing by pulled the two girls apart.

Although everyone congratulated her for

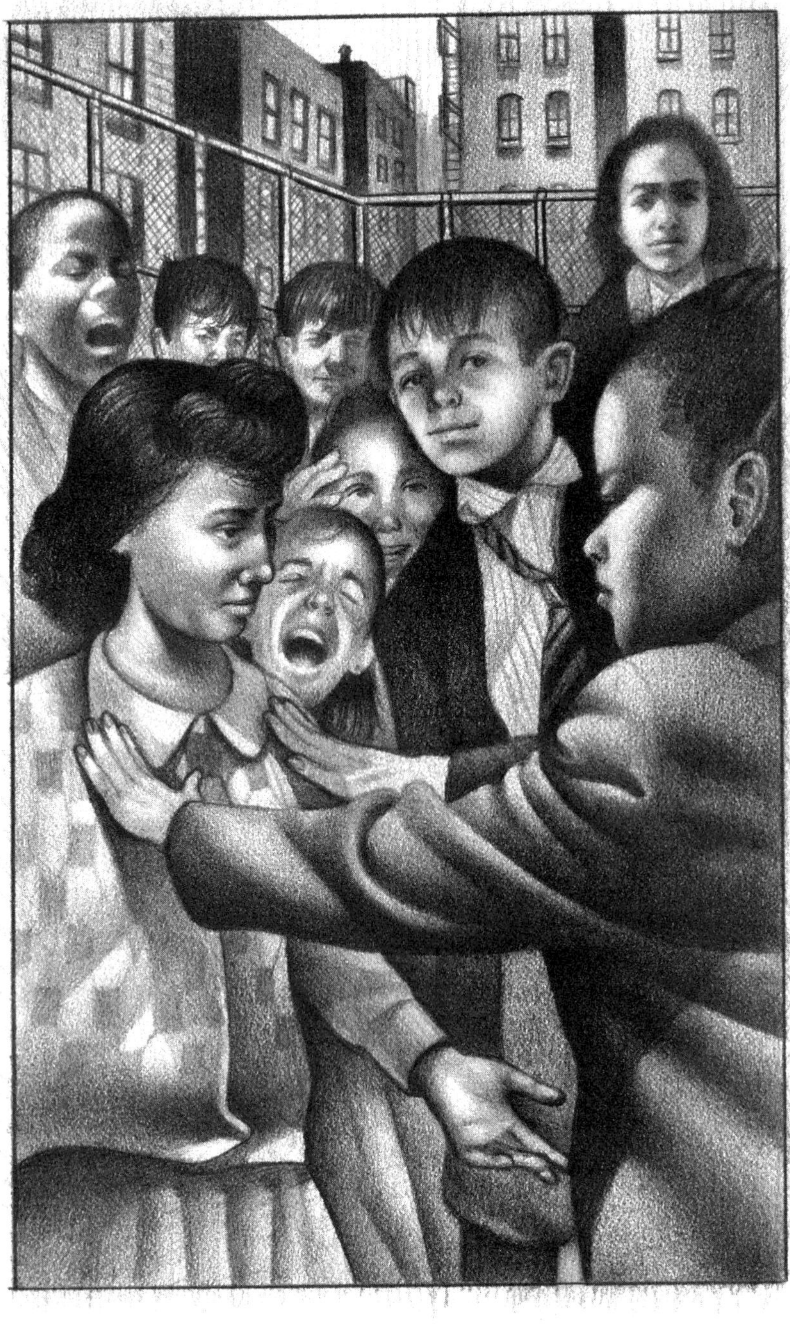

winning, Evelina felt bad. She wanted to know why people were so mean to each other. Why did they fight for nothing? When she told her aunt the story, she asked her a question. "Are those girls different from me because they're black?"

"No," answered Tía Vicenta. "We're all the same. In fact many of our ancestors in Puerto Rico were black men and women. They were brought in from Africa and forced to work as slaves. Just like here. So we are all the same, and we are all God's children."

Back in school Evelina said hello to the bully and her friend. To her surprise, they said hello back. It was a start. As time went on, the three girls made friends with each other. Evelina visited their homes and they visited hers.

Evelina's first year in New York City came and went. She was making friends, learning English, and doing better and better in school. But not a day passed that she didn't miss her mother and sisters. Each night

Evelina prayed that one day they would all be united so that she might have her family with her again.

Meanwhile, Evelina's household on 117th Street was growing. In order to bring in some additional income, Tía Vicenta and Tío Godreau rented their extra bedroom. Their tenant's name was Miriam, a young single parent with a baby boy. Evelina liked Miriam very much and loved the baby. She was always taking care of baby Jorgito when Miriam had to go out.

"You are such a big help, Evelina," Miriam said, thanking her. "I don't know how I could manage without you."

But for Evelina, helping with baby Jorgito made the separation from her mother and sisters less painful. "It is you and the baby who are helping me," she responded.

3 PEOPLE ARE HUNGRY

The Great Depression was hurting *El Barrio,* just as it was hurting the rest of the United States. Many people were out of work and unable to feed their families or themselves. Old clothes were repaired, not replaced. Who had money for a new coat or new gloves?

Empty stomachs and worn clothes made February 1935 seem even colder than usual. The Depression was in its sixth year, and people were struggling just to survive. Even those who had jobs, like Tía Vicenta and Tío Godreau, needed to find extra income to make ends meet.

To help those who were suffering the most, President Franklin Delano Roosevelt established food programs for the needy. Unemployed people and people earning very little money were given forms to fill out for extra food. Completed forms were exchanged for food packages at the distribution centers. The government packages included such basics as canned goods, flour, cereal, powdered milk, peanut butter, and cheese.

But to claim their food people had to complete and return the government forms. For some this wasn't so easy.

When Miriam lost her job, she refused to fill out the forms and go for her food. "I'm no charity case," said Miriam. "I don't want free handouts. I want to work and earn my food." She was not alone in thinking this way.

"It's too humiliating to go with a piece of paper in one's hand to ask for food . . . like a beggar," said their neighbor Señor Sanchez. "No, I can't—I won't—beg for food. No!"

But Evelina could see that many of these people were hungry. Their children went to school without having eaten breakfast. In the streets she saw people selling apples for pennies. She saw homeless people huddled in doorways. She saw people line up by the hundreds in front of soup kitchens waiting to eat. Yet her neighbors refused available food.

This made no sense to Evelina. Without help, Miriam, Jorgito, and Señor Sanchez might soon be huddled in doorways or on soup kitchen lines, too.

Evelina wanted to do something. Her mother had brought her up with a strong sense of right and wrong. Her mother used to tell her that people who work hard and pay taxes deserve some help from the government when times are difficult. The government should help those in need find jobs. It should, her mother said, make sure everyone can live a decent life.

If her mother was right, why did these people refuse to claim food that they needed and deserved? Evelina was confused, so she spoke to her aunt and uncle.

"People are hungry. They would work if

there were jobs, but there aren't any. Now they need food to nourish themselves and their families. They are wrong to refuse."

"Well," said Tío Godreau sadly, "most of them are too ashamed. They don't understand that it's not their fault. Sometimes I take the forms of one or two of our neighbors with me when I go get our food. As long as I'm there I can bring back a few items for them."

"Evelina," Tía Vicenta told her, "we Puerto Ricans are a proud people. We don't want to appear like beggars or charity cases. That's just the way we are. It's our nature. What can we do?"

"No!" answered Evelina. "That food belongs to the people and they should have it. Things must change."

"And who is going to change things, young lady?" asked Tío Godreau.

"I am," said Evelina, smiling. "And you, Tío, are going to help!"

Evelina also spoke to Miriam. "I know

how you feel about going for food. But you always talk about how much I help you with Jorgito. Now you must help me. Please come to the distribution center with me and Tío. Help us get the food. Remember, there are many hungry people out there."

Miriam thought about it. "Since I can see how determined you are to do this," said Miriam, "I'll go with you and Godreau."

That week Evelina went to visit as many of her neighbors as she could find who were entitled to food. "Fill out your forms," she told them. "I will get your food for you. Don't worry."

Some still weren't sure. "What if they won't give it to you?" asked Doña Josefina, who lived in a building across the street.

"Then you will be no worse off than you are now," answered Evelina. "But if it works, you will have food on your table."

"Suppose they expect us to come in next time?" another neighbor argued.

"I promise," answered Evelina, "I will go

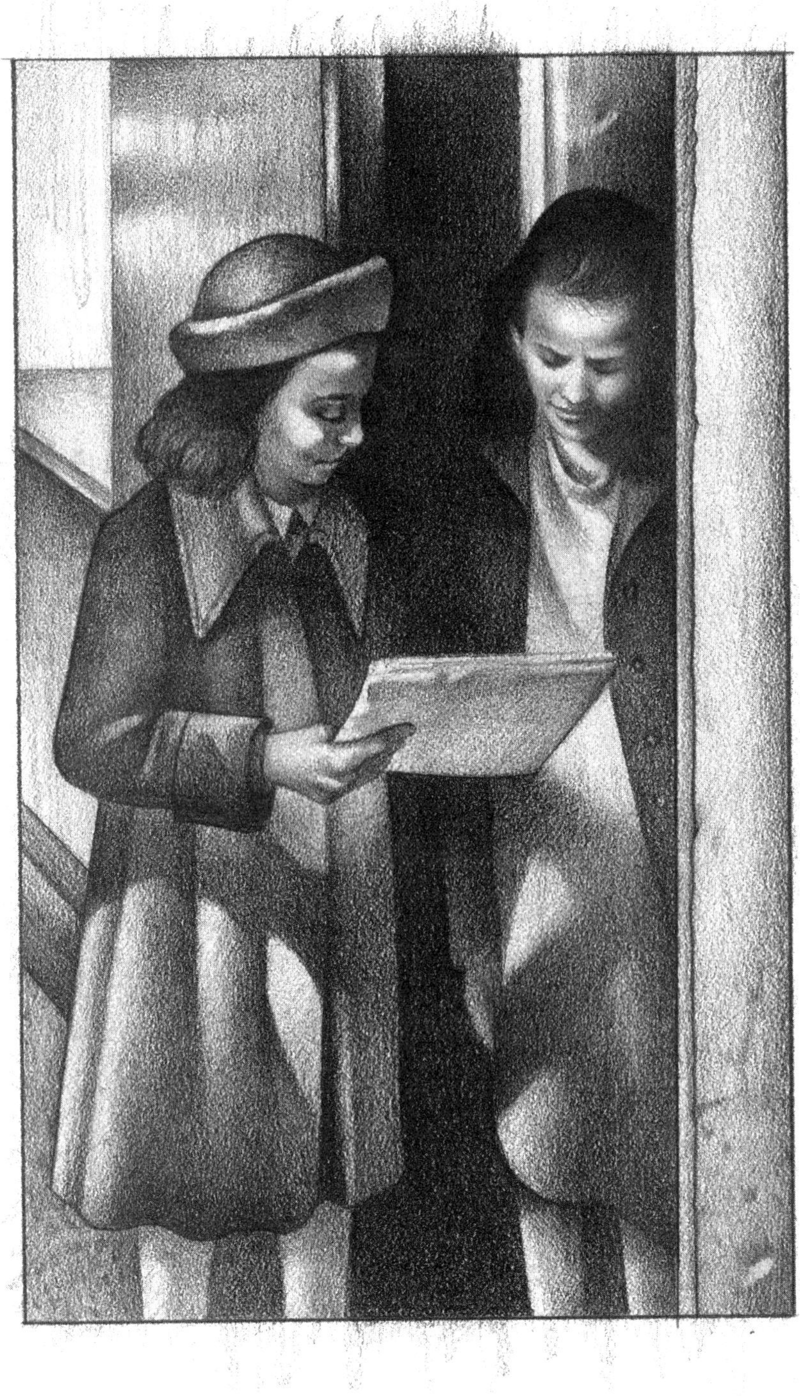

again and again and again." She was determined to help her neighbors. "Just fill out your forms and leave the rest to me."

Once Evelina had convinced her neighbors to give her their completed forms, she faced another big problem. The distribution center was located across town and several stops uptown as well. This meant at least a forty-minute trolley ride. How could she transport food for a dozen families such a long way with only Miriam and her uncle to help her?

"What about your Cousin Santos?" suggested Tía Vicenta. "Maybe he can help. He drives the trolley car that goes by the food center, and it stops right nearby on the corner of 116th Street."

Evelina spoke to Santos. Her cousin agreed to let Evelina bring the food on his trolley. But it would have to be on the last run when he was returning to the depot. It would be safer then because he would have no passengers. Any other time Santos would get caught using the trolley for personal business and lose his job.

Santos's last run was very late in the evening, long after the food center closed for the day. Once Evelina picked up the food, she would have a five-hour wait in the cold February weather. So now the problem was where to wait with the food until the trolley came.

Evelina visited a church that was near the food distribution center. She spoke to the minister about her plan to collect food for the poor. "We need your help, sir," she declared. "I will be taking many shopping bags of food to give to poor and hungry families. We'll have to wait for five hours before we can take it away, and it's very cold. Please help."

The minister was very impressed with little Evelina. He agreed to help her and ordered the sexton to let them wait with the food in the church basement until Santos came.

The day arrived and Evelina rode free on Santos's trolley to the food distribution center. When she presented the stack of completed forms at the counter, all the workers were taken aback.

"Where are all the people who claim this food?" asked the supervisor, who had been quickly called to the counter by one of the workers.

"They are too ashamed to come," Evelina answered. "They feel like they are begging, so I have come to get their food for them."

"This is too irregular," said the supervisor, shaking his head. "I don't know."

"Is there a law against this, sir? Doesn't the food belong to the people who filled out the forms? Isn't this food for poor families and their children?"

Evelina bombarded the supervisor with questions and statements.

"Plenty of people are starving and you have so much food here. If they can't come here to get it, then why can't I take it to

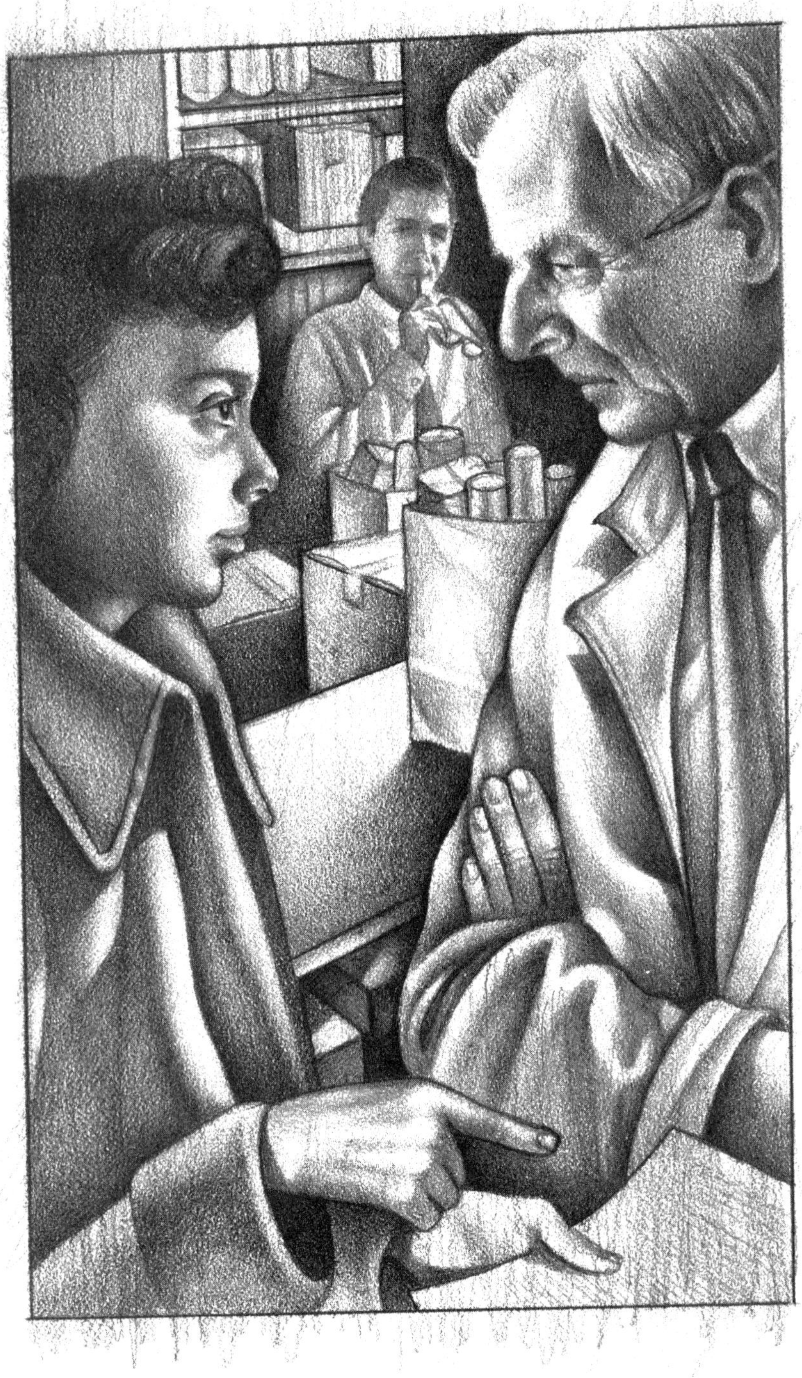

them? Please, sir," she pleaded, "in the name of justice! It's the only way, and it must be allowed!"

"You're wearing me out!" the supervisor complained with a laugh. "But even if I give you all of these shopping bags, how will you get them out of here?"

"My uncle and my neighbor will be here in one hour to help. Then we are delivering the shopping bags to each and every one of these families. Right to their door," she told him, "like I have promised them. I may come back every month. *¿Pero, quién sabe?* But who knows? Maybe some of these families will come here for themselves next time. Only don't worry because the people will get their food."

All the employees came out to see who this girl with the pretty face and dark, curly hair was. Evelina smiled happily as she checked out all the food against the completed forms. Then she took each shopping bag and set it against the wall and waited until she saw Tío Godreau and Miriam. They had each brought an empty wagon to the center.

"By God, you did it!" shouted Tío Godreau. Miriam hugged Evelina. "You are something special, little Miss Evelina!" she said.

All three loaded the shopping bags into the wagons. The wagons were not big enough to carry all twelve bags in one trip. So they made two trips to the nearby church before all the food was safely put into the church basement.

Then they waited for Santos and his trolley. Finally, in the darkness of night, they loaded the shopping bags onto the trolley. Santos shut off the lights inside the trolley. Then he told them that they must sit way in the back of the trolley.

"You three will have to keep down and stay out of sight," said Santos. "I'll be passing by all the trolley stops. But," he added nervously, "if another driver—or our dispatcher—sees you, I'll be in trouble. So stay low!"

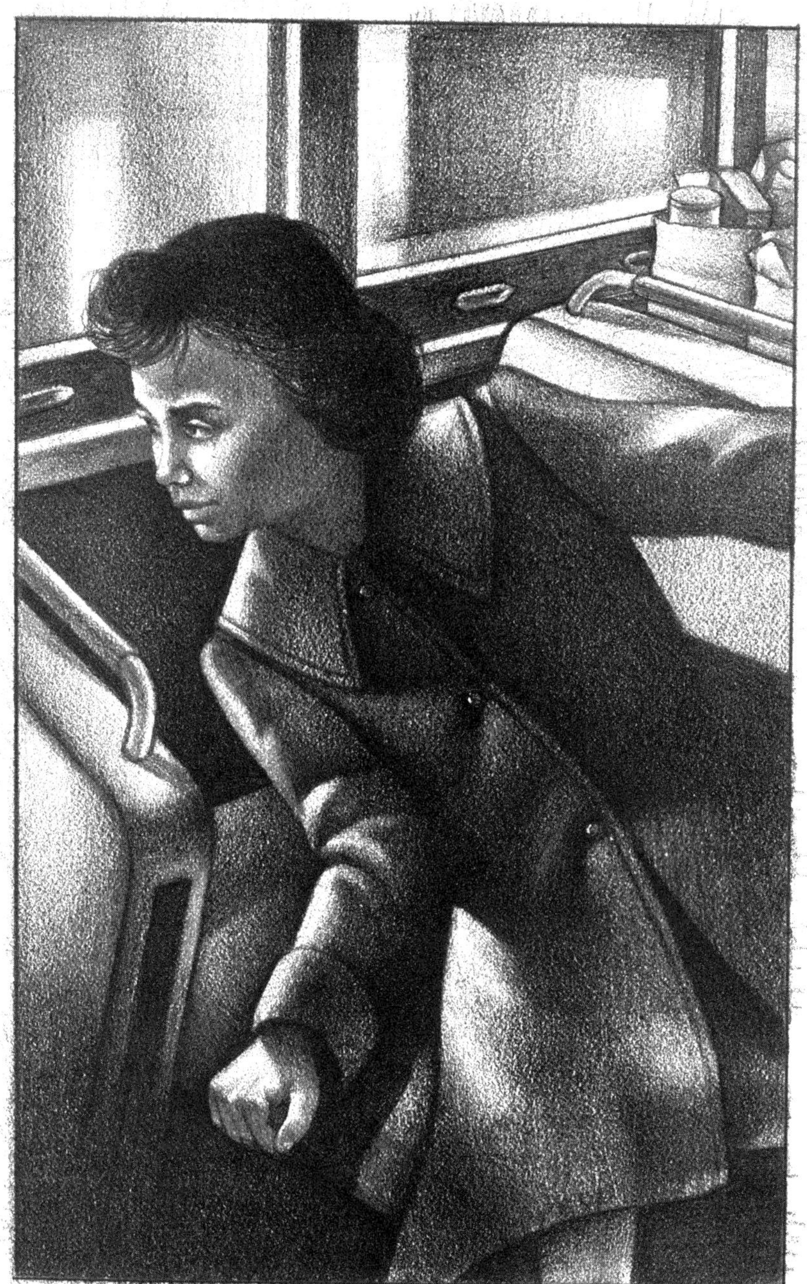

Evelina, Tío Godreau, and Miriam sat scrunched down in the shadows at the back of the trolley. Each time they passed a trolley stop, they heard Santos say a prayer under his breath. When they finally reached 116th Street, Evelina felt a sense of relief just knowing that Cousin Santos would not be in trouble.

That night Evelina, Tío Godreau, and Miriam went to the door of every family that had completed a form and distributed the food to them.

On her next trip to the distribution center, Evelina was not alone. She was joined by a group of neighbors, including Señor Sanchez.

"Evelina, you've given us courage," he told her. "From now on I'll be going to get my own food and so will the rest of us."

With each passing month, Evelina's task of collecting food became easier. More and more of her neighbors went to the distribution center with her.

Soon all her neighbors were seeking on their own the help they were entitled to.

Evelina had shown her neighbors that there was no shame in accepting help when it was needed. Babies wouldn't cry through the night for food. Children wouldn't go to school hungry and with no energy to learn. And people working or looking for work wouldn't get sick because they didn't have enough food to eat.

4 UNO, DOS, TRES

Despite the hard times of the Depression, Tía Vicenta and Tío Godreau had never forgotten about Evelina's mother and sisters. From the day Evelina had arrived, they had saved any extra money they could spare for the fares to bring Evelina's family to New York.

Evelina had done her best to help, too.

Each morning and each night, she prayed that her family would be reunited. During the day she searched for empty cans and bottles to cash in for their deposits. She saved every penny of the deposit money. She kept the money in a sealed jar in the back of a drawer in her bureau. Slowly the pennies began filling the jar. Too slowly, thought Evelina.

Evelina went to her aunt and uncle. "Tell me," she pleaded, "what else I can do to help get money for Mami and Lilli and the baby to get here?"

"Some of our neighbors could use the help of an interpreter. Maybe you could earn money that way," suggested Tío Godreau.

"After all, your English is very good," added Tía Vicenta.

They were both right. Her English was very good indeed. Evelina began to help her neighbors who didn't speak English by acting as their interpreter. She went with people to clinics and city agencies to help them fill out forms and to talk to clerks behind the counters.

Most of the people she helped were poor, but they gave Evelina whatever they could spare. Neighbors began to rely on Evelina even when they couldn't pay for her help. Evelina never refused. She understood how poor everyone was. But people knew that Evelina wanted her family to come to New York, so if they had any money at all, they'd press a penny or two into her hands.

"Here's a little something to help," they'd tell her.

Evelina saved everything she earned, and the money began to add up more quickly.

Every night she would empty the jar out and count, *uno, dos, tres.* . . . "One, two, three. . . ." By March of 1935, a month after her first visit to the food distribution center, she had saved ten dollars.

When she took the money to her aunt and uncle, they were surprised and very moved. With all the hubbub over the food distribution center the month before, they had almost forgotten that Evelina was saving her money.

"Listen," said Tío Godreau, "we were not going to tell you this right away, but. . . ." He hesitated, then smiled. "Your aunt and I will be sending some money to your mother very

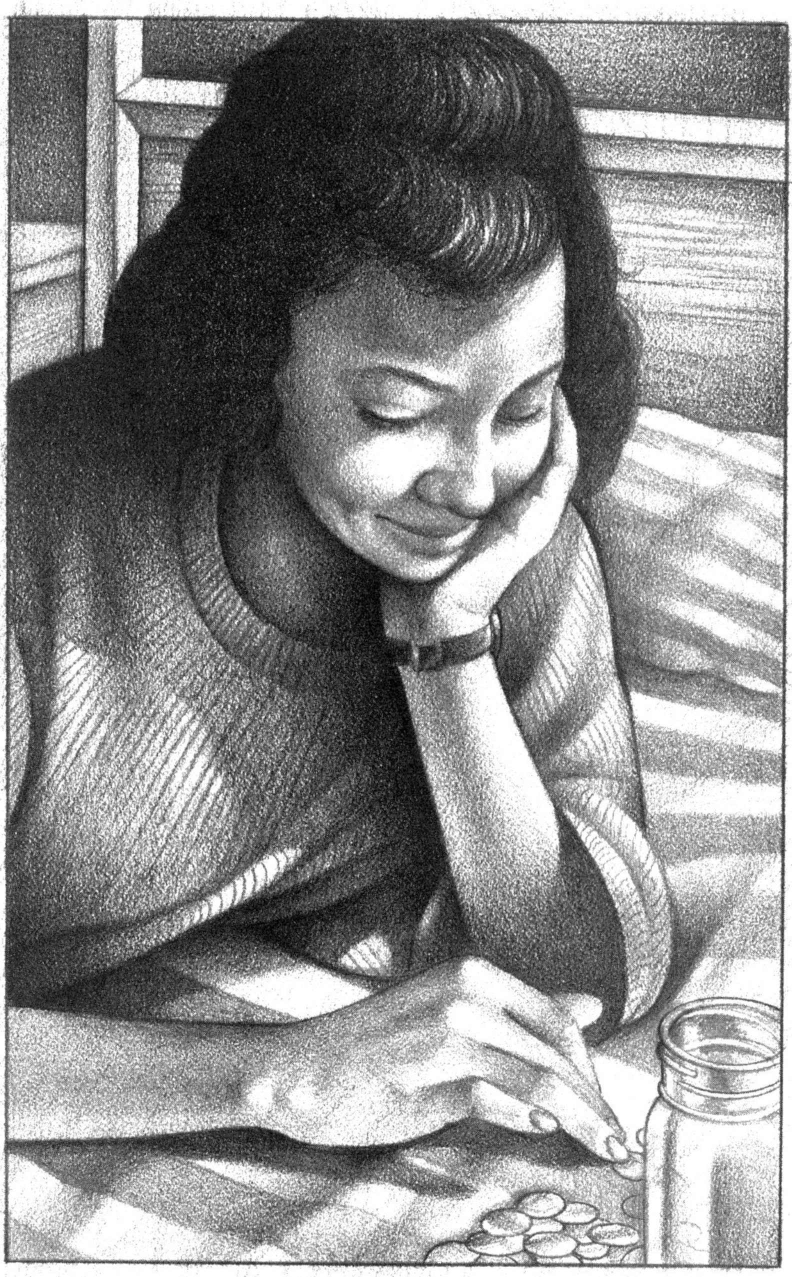

soon. Together with the money your mother has saved, there is finally enough for the fares. She and Lillian and baby Elba will be coming to live with us by May."

On hearing the news, Evelina thought her heart would burst with happiness. She would finally have her mother and her sisters with her. She ached to see them, touch them, and feel complete with her family around her once more.

"You keep that money," said her aunt, "and just before they get here we will go shopping for some nice presents for them."

Two months later on May 20, 1935, just about a year and a half after her own arrival, Evelina once again stood on the South Brooklyn docks. This time, though, she was filled with joy. She stood at the front of an excited crowd waiting for the passengers to disembark from the very ship that had brought her to New York, *El Ponce*.

"Do you see them?" asked Tía Vicenta.

"Not yet," answered Evelina, tears of happiness clouding her eyes.

Tío Godreau saw Evelina's watery eyes. "It's hard," he said, "from so far away to see anyone's face." Evelina wiped away her tears and gave her uncle a grateful smile.

Then she quickly returned to the search for her family among the crowd of passengers. The gangplank was down, and people were streaming off the ship. Then she saw them! Mami, Lillian, and baby Elba! They stepped off the gangplank and hurried toward Evelina, who was now shouting and waving.

"Mami, you're here!" she cried.

Mi hijita, que mucha falta me has hecho. "How much I have missed you, my sweet daughter," her mother said, hugging Evelina. Evelina welcomed her mother's words and long embrace.

Then Evelina hugged Lillian and whispered, *Tengo tanto que contarte.* "I have so much to tell you." It was good to have her sister Lillian close to her. Now she had someone to confide in. Finally she picked up baby Elba and kissed her. "I might have missed

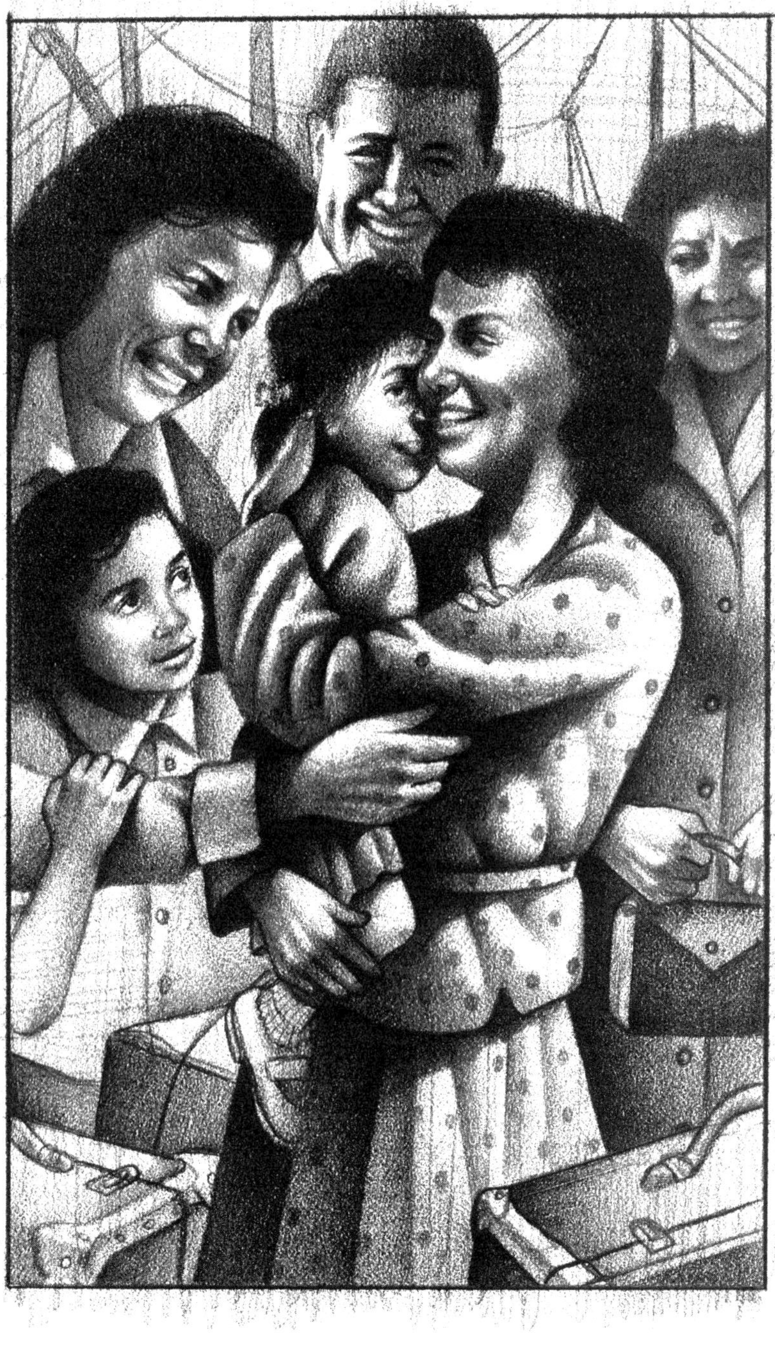

your first steps but from now on you will always have your big sister by your side."

"Well, Vicenta and Godreau," said Evelina's mother, "I want to thank you for taking care of my daughter and giving her a good home. I hope she has been a help to you, too."

"Eva, are you serious?" asked Godreau, laughing. "Since Evelina's arrival nothing will ever be the same again. Everywhere we go people know your daughter." Tío Godreau hesitated and smiled. "Goodness, I can't owe money anymore because now my creditors can always find me! Everyone knows where that Evelina who brought food to the community lives!" Eva laughed at Tío Godreau's joke and gave Evelina another big hug.

"Life will never be the same around here," Tío Godreau added, with a wink for Evelina. "And it's all for the better."

Epilogue

Tío Godreau was proven to be right. By caring about others and taking the initiative, Evelina had helped her neighbors. And she continued to change things for the better for the rest of her life.

In high school a classmate of Evelina's became ill and was sent to the school infirmary. No one was on duty in the infirmary. The sick girl sat alone and scared without any treatment or help. When Evelina found out, she became so angry that she decided to do something about it. She persuaded several students to stay out of school in protest. This small boycott was effective. Soon after, a nurse was in attendance at the school infirmary.

A few years later, Evelina organized a larger boycott—one against neighborhood stores. Most of the customers in these stores were either Puerto Rican or African American. But the white storeowners continually refused to hire any people of color to work in the stores.

Evelina decided that two could play at the game of refusal. She rallied her neighbors, and they stopped shopping in those stores. The stores changed their hiring practices. And it was all for the better.

Later, after she married and had children of her own, Evelina joined the Parent-Teacher Association of her children's school. It was the middle of the 1960s, and she was living in a part of New York City called the South Bronx. This was one of the city's poorest and most run-down areas. Even some of the people who lived and worked there called it a "bad neighborhood."

But Evelina felt differently. She insisted her children's school provide the best education it could for the children of the neighborhood. But Evelina found that no matter what issue she raised, school officials wouldn't listen to her. Outraged, she called a meeting of parents and friends in the community and told them how it was.

"They don't respect us as parents. These school officials don't want anyone to tell them that they're doing a terrible job. All they want is a PTA that's interested in 'tea and cakes,'" she told them. "Not one of these officials has a real idea of what it takes to give our children a good education!"

Evelina quit the PTA and began talking with parents outside the school grounds. Many told her how unhappy they were and how badly their children were being treated.

"These teachers do not expect much from our children because they are Puerto Rican," one told her.

"They expect them to do poorly," said another.

"In school they are punished for speaking Spanish," said a third.

Evelina listened. She agreed with all that she heard. The situation was disgraceful. Soon she had organized the parents into a volunteer committee. They called themselves the United Bronx Parents. At first they only worked in one school. But in no time they had members from all over the South Bronx.

At first they tried to work with the schools and with city officials. But again no one listened. So the United Bronx Parents took action. They held protest marches. They called local politicians and television and newspaper reporters. They showed them firsthand how poor conditions were in the schools of the South Bronx. Calls to the Board of Education from upset politicians, and unflattering stories on TV and in the papers embarrassed school officials. This led to positive changes. Once more Evelina had made a difference.

The United Bronx Parents with Evelina as its president continued to make progress.

UNITED BRONX PARENTS, INC.
FOR GOOD EDUCATION IN OUR COMMUNITY
SPONSORED BY OEO N.Y. URBAN COALITION

Their efforts led to a program of healthier lunches, better training for teachers, and understanding and cooperation between parents and school officials. Special educational programs for Spanish-speaking students and better testing programs were also established. And many other good changes were made in the schools of the South Bronx.

Everyone benefited—the schools, the neighborhood, and the children.

Today the United Bronx Parents, under the direction of Lorraine Montenegro, carries forth the legacy of Evelina Lopez Antonetty. It works to improve education in the public schools and to make life better for the people of the South Bronx.

Afterword

The story of Evelina Lopez Antonetty (1922–1984), is the story of a Puerto Rican woman who showed herself over and over again to be a leader. She proved that one person could make a difference. It was her faith in humanity and her love of all people that helped her succeed. She is remembered by people in the South Bronx and throughout the larger Puerto Rican community.

Evelina's story was told with the help of her sisters, Lillian Lopez and Elba Cabrera, and her daughter Lorraine Montenegro. Additional information came from several recorded interviews with Evelina that were made available to us through the kind cooperation of the Center for Puerto Rican Studies at Hunter College in New York City. The conversations in quotations are based on those recalled in the stories told by or about Evelina.

Notes

Page 2 Evelina's family lived in Salinas, Puerto Rico, and later moved to Ponce. Salinas is a fishing village, Ponce a large city. Both are on Puerto Rico's southern coast. Salinas is about twenty miles east of Ponce.

Page 2 The hard times of the Depression forced many people to leave their homes in search of better opportunities. Few found them. The Depression hit all parts of the country hard, so people usually found things to be just as bad or only a little better where they moved.

Pages 11–12 Many people mistakenly think that Puerto Ricans in the United States are immigrants. But immigrants are people who leave one country to live in another. Puerto Rico has been part of the United States since 1898. The people of the Commonwealth of Puerto Rico have been United States citizens since 1917.

Puerto Ricans began coming to New York City as early as the 1800s. (Puerto Rico was still a Spanish colony then, so people who came in those early years of migration were immigrants.) In 1918, right after World War I ended, came the first significant wave of migration from Puerto Rico to New York City. It continued right up to the start of World War II. When the war ended in 1945, the largest wave of Puerto Rican migration began, lasting into the 1950s and 1960s.

Today, thanks to air travel, Puerto Ricans frequently travel back and forth to the Island.

Page 21 Evelina's ancestors may have included the Taino people, who were the original native settlers on the Island of Puerto Rico, as well as the Spaniards who came from Europe and the Africans who were brought from Africa.

Christopher Columbus explored Puerto Rico on his second voyage in 1493. It is the only part of the modern-day United States that was visited by Columbus on his four voyages. Ponce de León established the first Spanish settlement in 1508, one hundred years before Jamestown was founded by the English. The first Africans were brought to Puerto Rico as slaves in 1510.

For many years Puerto Rico fought for its independence from Spain, but the Island remained a Spanish colony until 1898.

Pages 23–24 The Depression lasted from the late 1920s into the 1940s. It was the worst period of unemployment and poverty in our country's history. Many Americans were like Miriam in feeling too ashamed to accept "charity." They did not want to admit they were poor and hungry. Many blamed themselves. They would search and search for work and still blame themselves when there were no available jobs.

All through the Depression poor people suffered from sicknesses caused by a lack of food and proper health care. The many homeless people suffered the most. They lived in doorways or cardboard boxes and had little protection against cold and wet weather.

Page 48 Evelina's belief in education was very strong. In 1964 she worked as a coordinator for Head Start in the Bronx, preparing young children for school. Under her leadership the United Bronx Parents became very involved not only in education of children but also in adult-literacy programs.

During the mid-1970s, Evelina organized a "sit-in" at the Tremont Avenue branch of the New York Public Library to protest library closings in poor neighborhoods. Evelina told her supporters, "We can't let them close our libraries." She demanded that city officials explain themselves to the people of the South Bronx. "How can you take from us when we have so little?"

The group occupied the library for several weeks. Many of the demonstrators spent time reading as they waited for a resolution to their protest. Evelina and her supporters were very careful to do no damage to any of the books or to library property during the long demonstration. "We left that place cleaner than we found it," she said later. The sit-in was successful, and several branches marked for closing were kept open.

Nicholasa Mohr is an award-winning writer and artist. Ms. Mohr's many books for children include *Felita, Going Home,* and *Nilda.*